# MAGNUS LEADERSHIP:
## Greatness with Purpose

Mission:   To Proclaim Transformation and Truth
Publisher: Transformed Publishing, Cocoa, FL
Website:   www.transformedpublishing.com
Email:     transformedpublishing@gmail.com

Magnus Leadership logo provided by author. All other interior and accent images were retrieved by the publisher, via paid subscription / terms of use from Storyblocks.

This work is based on the author's life experiences and personal Biblical study, prayer, and inspiration of the Holy Spirit. The intention of the author is to share his testimony, insight, and strategies that have helped him, in hope to inspire others. Any resemblance to someone else's life experiences, teaching, actual events or locales or persons, living or dead, is entirely coincidental.

ISBN: 978-1-953241-81-8 (paperback)
ISBN: 978-1-953241-82-5 (hardcover)
ISBN: 978-1-953241-83-2 (ebook)

# MAGNUS LEADERSHIP:
## Greatness with Purpose

MICHAEL A. CADORE, Ed.D.

Servant & Catalytic Leader│Community Advocate│Educator

# MAGNUS SOLUTIONS, INC.

"Not just good ideas, but MAGNUS SOLUTIONS!"

"If you don't serve your community now,
don't expect your community to serve you later."

- Michael A. Cadore, Ed. D
Founder & President
Magnus Solutions, Inc

# Dedication

To my family, mentors, students,
teammates, and colleagues,
you are the reason this book exists.

To the countless community members,
law-enforcement partners, educators, and students
who have walked with me, this is for you.

May every reader find purpose, power,
and peace through service.

# Acknowledgements

Cornelia, my beloved wife, my queen, thank you for standing beside me through every season of life.

Anthony V. Cadore Sr, my late father, and my grandfather, Magnus Cadore, whose names and values breathe through every page. Your legacies remind me daily that greatness is not about being seen, it's about serving.

My beloved brothers: Jeff, Gary, Tony, and Joseph; thankfully, we all grew up under one roof. Their loyalty, accountability, and unwavering support shaped my understanding of leadership long before titles or platforms. Through shared challenges and victories, they taught me that true leadership begins with respect for family, for purpose, and for one another. Their lives and love remind me that greatness is never achieved alone, but through unity, trust, and standing together with integrity. Jeff, my oldest brother and hero, set the standard early by demonstrating what strength and responsibility truly look like. Gary (deceased 2002), the protector, provided security, confidence, and steady guidance through every season. Tony, truly my first best friend, the singer and military brother, modeled discipline and faith, offering prayers and counsel that guided my decisions and sharpened my purpose. Joseph, my baby brother, continues to remind me of the power of loyalty, heart, and authenticity, and of family bonds that never fade.

Anthony "Mitch" Mitchell, my childhood friend, a natural leader even at nine years old, recruited me to join his team. Our fathers both served as police officers in our city, embodying service and integrity. Anthony was our quarterback, true leader guiding us to youth league championships and eventually two unforgettable high school state titles with a team full of greatness. To this day, Anthony and I continue to serve together in the community; proof that brotherhood and purpose don't end with the game; they evolve through service."

My EKU parents, I honor you both, Mary "Momma V" and Charles aka "Doc" Veurink, whose love, guidance, and generosity embraced me far beyond the classroom and the field. Outside of being our team doctor, they provided stability, encouragement, and a sense of home that strengthened my spirit and sharpened my focus.

Their steadfast belief in me reinforced the importance of compassion, accountability, and family principles that continue to guide my leadership journey. I am forever grateful for the role they played in shaping not only my collegiate experience, but the man and leader I continue to become.

## Magnus Leadership
### *Built Through Family, Faith, and Service*

Every one of you contributed to the framework and foundation Magnus Leadership is built on. I am eternally thankful for the opportunity to continue moving *our* legacy forward by investing in the next generation.

# Endorsements

Senator Bill Posey,
*Former Florida Senate and U.S. House of Representatives*

I have always believed that good leadership begins with an individual's unwavering desire to serve others, and the willingness to put the needs of others before their own.

Thankfully, we see servant heart leadership every day. Sometimes it manifests in government, military service, business culture, and sometimes even in politics. But most of all, when you look around our communities, there are servant heart leaders making a difference in people's lives through their churches, through outreach and charitable work, general self-less acts of kindness, and generosity to others in need, without any expectation of personal benefit.

Servant heart leaders work together to strengthen the fabric of communities, and their acts set an example for others to follow.

I believe you possess such qualities, Michael Cadore.

Joe Mirachi,
*Launch Credit Union*

Michael, you are gifted at connecting with people and building relationships that elevate others. When you interact with someone, you naturally give them your full attention, making them feel not just heard but valued. Time and again, I have seen you lead with empathy yet follow through with decisive actions that solve problems. In summary, you have a knack for bringing out the best in others as you accomplish great things together.

Samantha Lopez-Bickman,
*Vice President of U.T.B. United Third Bridge, Inc.*

Dr. Cadore is a committed leader who has made significant contributions to our community over the past decade. His dedication to education, service, and leadership has positively impacted students, families, and professionals in Brevard County and beyond. Through his work with Eastern Florida State College, MAGNUS Solutions Inc., and various community initiatives, Michael has created opportunities for growth, connection, and success.

His professionalism and generosity consistently benefit our mission. Recognizing him as an Ambassador via U.T.B. United Third Bridge highlights his purposeful servant leadership and lasting influence on many lives. Thank you, Michael, for your commitment and inspiring guidance.

-Submitted with deep gratitude and respect.

Jackie Colon,
*Executive Coach, Maxwell Leadership Team*

Michael, you are a man of great character and integrity. Over the past two decades, I have watched you lead with purpose, humility, and empathy, whether as a football coach guiding a young 13-year-old or as a police officer and dedicated public servant. You have truly walked the walk. You have never forgotten where you come from.

Good leadership must begin with empathy and compassion for those we lead. That is where trust is built. As an Executive Coach and Leadership Trainer, I have learned that it's not just about having IQ, but also EQ, emotional intelligence which allows us to connect, understand, and effectively lead.

-Respectfully submitted, knowing this book will bring value to people.

Sandy Handfield,

*Associate Vice President of Academic Affairs EFSC*
*(Eastern Florida State College)*

Leadership, to me, is not a title or a position. It is a daily commitment to serve, to listen, and to act with integrity even when no one is watching. My journey through education, community engagement, and public service here in Brevard County has taught me that the most meaningful leadership begins with humility. It is rooted in relationships, strengthened by trust, and sustained by a genuine desire to leave people and communities better than we found them. Good leaders create space for others to grow, remain steady in times of challenge, and never lose sight of the greater good.

Michael's leadership journey reflects these values in action. What I have consistently observed in him is a rare blend of purpose, compassion, and account-ability. He leads with clarity, but also with heart; taking the time to understand people, elevate their voices, and empower them to succeed. Michael does not seek recognition; instead, he focuses on impact. His decisions are thoughtful, his standards are high, and his commitment to service is unwavering. He leads by example, demonstrating that strong leadership is as much about character as it is about competence.

To the students, professionals, and community servants who read this: let Michael's example remind you that leadership is service in motion. Lead with courage, listen with intention, and act with kindness. When you center your leadership on people and purpose, your influence will extend far beyond your role, and your legacy will be felt long after the work is done.

Jeff Davis (Oldest Brother),
*North Area Manager Brevard Parks and Recreation*

> "The tip of the arrow is sharp,
> but the blade must be strong."

Michael, my younger brother, I knew from day one that all I needed to do was move forward in the right direction as the oldest child, and you would follow with strength. I am profoundly proud of you, with no envy, only pure love.

As a leader, you must realize that you are always providing an example. What you teach others isn't always what you say, but what you do.

Your book is purposeful. I started writing my grand-children memos and little notes of encouragement, so I deeply understand the importance of what you are doing. Hopefully, the sharing of my wisdom will make your task easier.

My Phi Beta Sigma Fraternity line name and our beloved cousin "Oz" come to mind. That word means strength, might, power, and courage.

Michael, know yourself and be true to who you are and what you believe. These are the attributes needed to be a truly effective leader. Continue to lead, teach, and inspire.

Dr. Brenda Fettrow,
*Rockledge City Manager*

Dr. Cadore posed the question, "What does good leadership mean to me?" It means having integrity and character, that no matter how difficult a decision or action may be, always doing the right thing ... whatever is best for the organization and/or employer ... not yourself.

In making hiring decisions, I have always said, "Hire people with good character and core values because that is NOT something that you can teach; but you can teach people to conduct business aligned with policy and procedures.

I have always said, "I have worked my entire career to build my reputation, character, and integrity, so I'm not compromising it for anything or anybody. It's too hard to earn. Just a few nuggets. Thank you for the opportunity to share. I am deeply honored!

Honorable Judge Kimberly Musselman,
*Brevard County Judge*

Michael is a leader who empowers people to strive for excellence in their personal and professional lives through positivity, humor, and a genuine celebration of life's victories. He accomplishes this by truly listening to ideas, goals, and challenges alike. With both heart and mind, he instills the resilience needed to overcome setbacks. His impactful interactions, no matter how brief, are uplifting and deeply meaningful to the people he serves.

Max King,
*President Brevard Community College (1968 to 1988)*

When it comes to the decision-making process, it is important to gather the best information available and get the best people to give you their opinions on the issue you are attempting to address. Always base your decision on what action is going to help people the most in the long run and then move forward.

The only way to lead is to lead. Our community continually benefits from the stellar leadership of Dr. Michael Cadore and those who he has mentored along the way as an extension of his service.

Coach Leon Hart,
*Eastern Kentucky University Football Offensive Coordinator*

Good leadership, to me, is not being afraid to speak up for what you believe in and at the same time setting an example for those words through your actions.

Michael, it was evident very early in your time with us at EKU that you were focused on being the very best player and student you could be. Your work ethic and dedication were obvious from the beginning.

Being vocal, at first, was not your natural approach. Presenting a positive example and showcasing your exemplary character was perfect for you. Other players gravitated to you and were willing to follow your lead.

As you became more comfortable in your new environment the vocal aspect stepped up but always accompanied by a great example. *Do as I say and do as I do,* both fit your leadership style.

The outstanding success you had as a player that carries on in your professional career is not a surprise to any of us who know you. Your life as a player, husband, father, co-worker and community leader are all a continuation of your ability to inspire others.

You set a high bar for people but it's obvious to them that your willingness to reach ever higher in your own life motivates them to believe that they can reach these lofty goals.

Watching your life as it progresses and develops is very gratifying to me as one of your former teachers and coaches.

# Table of Contents

# Introduction
## The Journey of a Servant Leader

Every season of my life has been guided by one unwavering truth: *leadership begins with service.*

From the football field to law enforcement, from higher education to public office, the call to lead has always been rooted in the commitment to *help others rise.*

Leadership isn't about titles. It's about impact. It's not about being the loudest voice in the room; it's about being the one who *listens* and *acts* with integrity.

In these pages, I share the principles that have shaped my journey. Lessons learned through victories, setbacks, mentorship, and faith.

These aren't theories. They're lived experiences forged on the front lines of community engagement, family, and personal growth.

Each chapter will reveal a **Principle of Success**, beginning with *Preparation* and ending with *Raise*, a call to lift others as you climb.

Along the way, you'll find **Magnus Nuggets**, which are brief reflections and actions designed to educate, encourage, and empower you right where you are.

Original Quote by Michael A. Cadore, Ed.D. Copyright © 2025

As you read, pause often. Reflect deeply. Because this book isn't just about my story. It's about yours. Take time to breathe in as you read.

> Before seeking applause, I just wanna thank You, Lord. True greatness is measured by the broken bridges you helped others cross.
>
> -Cadore's Magnus Nugget

## Reflection Questions:

1. Who are you currently serving? Why?
2. How do your daily actions reflect your personal definition of success?

1

3. What legacy do you want your leadership to leave behind?

_____

_____

_____

_____

_____

_____

_____

_____

_____

_____

_____

_____

_____

_____

_____

_____

_____

_____

_____

# Magnus Leadership

Leadership is not a position, it is a calling shaped by experience, adversity, accountability, and service. My journey began long before Eastern Kentucky University (EKU), long before professional football, long before law enforcement. It began in a home shaped by discipline, faith, and legacy. My father, Anthony V. Cadore Sr., and my grandfather Magnus laid the foundation for what I would later call *Magnus Leadership*, anchored in humility, preparation, and responsibility.

Being born in Titusville, Florida, I carried with me the Cadore name and the expectation to honor it. At Titusville High School, I joined a football program that demanded excellence. Those championship years were more than athletics; they were lessons in teamwork, consistency, and competing with character. Those early experiences prepared me for a future I didn't yet see being part of. The value of preparation grew more evident as we went on to be a state-championship program, earning 1,573 all-purpose yards my senior year, and learning what it meant to be accountable to a team larger than myself.

Eastern Kentucky University expanded that foundation. Under strong coaching and a culture built on discipline, I grew physically, mentally, and spiritually.

While at EKU, I earned First-Team All-Ohio Valley Conference honors, set an NCAA Division I-AA (FCS) Championship Game record with 232 kickoff return yards, and established a school record with a 30.3-yard career kickoff return average, a mark that remains among the program's best. Collegiate excellence led to my induction into the Eastern Kentucky University Athletics Hall of Fame

Being drafted by the New Orleans Saints and later competing in the World League of American Football with the Montreal Machine, finishing second in kickoff-return average taught me resilience, gratitude, and perspective. Especially, after an unexpected knee injury early in my professional football career, during a scrimmage game playing for the New Orleans Saints, resulting in surgery and rehabilitation. This humbled me but also refined me for a monumental comeback. While you may not have suffered a physical injury, most people experience discouragement at some point and must pivot to overcome setbacks.

Service continues to define me and has led me into influential positions at Eastern Florida State College, Launch Credit Union, and the Rockledge City Council.

The Magnus Leadership Principles of Success presented in this book are not a checklist, they are a compass. Every time you read this book, you will discover a new layer of your own leadership journey. Return to these pages often. Highlight your lessons. Write in the margins. Use the reflection spaces as mirrors of your growth. Magnus Leadership begins within and lives on through those you serve.

# Part I:
# Principles of Success

## Principle 1 – Preparation

Preparation is the unseen work that determines the outcome long before the moment arrives. In my life, preparation began early: before football, before college, and before public service. Preparation started with values: respect, responsibility, and remembering that whatever you do, you represent your family, your name, and your community. Preparation was the expectation in my home. My father, Anthony V. Cadore Sr., taught consistency, discipline, and honoring your commitments.

At Titusville High School, preparation was not optional. The coaches built a culture where success on Friday nights was earned on Monday mornings. The discipline of early practices, film study, conditioning, and team accountability shaped the leader I would become. It was not just about athletic talent, it was about mental readiness and a willingness to work when others rested.

Eastern Kentucky University took preparation to another level. Practices were faster, expectations higher, and the competition stronger. I learned that preparation meant studying opponents, mastering details, and conditioning myself to push through fatigue. It meant being coachable, being consistent, and never letting temporary discomfort stop long-term development.

A key component of preparation is to be able to look further down the road of life than your current location. I continued to advance athletically into the professional football arena, while knowing my academic preparation was even more essential for my future career and community service. As much as I continue to benefit from and value the disciplines of football, I always knew it was temporary and more so preparation for greater acceleration.

I'm grateful to Coach Al Werneke and Coach Jose Garcia who shaped my foundation, and Coach Roy Kidd who sharpened it to a championship standard The underlying core characteristics that built me into a record setting athlete have molded me into a valued community leader, holding essential positions, such as: trusted law enforcement officer, an essential part of the Eastern Florida State College leadership team, a noble Associate Board Member for Launch Credit Union, and a revered city councilman (Rockledge City Council Seat 1).

Original Quote by Michael A. Cadore, Ed.D. Copyright © 2025

The time you spend rehearsing in the shadow is the only deposit that guarantees confidence when the stadium lights turn on.

-Cadore's Magnus Nugget

## Reflection Questions:

1. How prepared are you for the opportunities you're praying for?
2. What small daily routines strengthen your readiness?
3. Who helps keep you accountable to your goals?

_____

_____

_____

_____

_____

_____

_____

_____

_____

_____

_____

_____

_____

_____

_____

_____

_____

_____

_____

_____

_____

_____

_____

_____

_____

## Principle 2 – Patience

Patience is one of the most misunderstood leadership qualities. For many, patience sounds like passiveness, waiting quietly, accepting delays, or tolerating discomfort. But true patience, the kind that has shaped every major step of my journey, is active, disciplined, and strategic. Patience is not sitting back; it is standing firm.

In my early years at Titusville High School, patience was something I learned unintentionally at first. On championship-level teams, everyone wants to shine, everyone wants to contribute, everyone wants their moment. But those teams taught me that patience is part of excellence. Waiting your turn, supporting your teammates, learning the system, respecting the structure, those were the seeds planted long before I understood their long-term impact.

At Eastern Kentucky University, patience took on a deeper meaning. The competition was tougher, the expectations higher, and the pressure real. I had to trust the process, trust my preparation, and trust that I would grow into the player I was meant to be. That trust paid off with All-OVC (Ohio Valley Conference) honors, record-breaking performances, and the opportunity to compete at the professional level. But none of that came overnight.

When the New Orleans Saints drafted me, I felt the weight of both opportunity and destiny. However, in one moment, life dealt an unexpected knee injury which tested everything I believed about leadership, character, and resilience. I had a choice like everyone confronted by opposition: become frustrated, bitter, and defeated ... or stay patient, stay committed, and stay ready for whatever came next. I remembered this was a game I was never expected to play at any level due to my health (asthma) and being under-sized.

Patience became my strength. It allowed me to heal. It allowed me to rebuild. And ultimately, it allowed me to take the field again. This time in the World League of American Football with the Montreal Machine. Finishing second in the league in kickoff-return average wasn't just a statistic; it was evidence that patience produces purpose.

Later, patience played a major role in my shift into public service. When I entered law enforcement, I learned quickly that many situations require listening more than reacting. High-risk encounters, community tension, and moments of crisis all required a level of emotional discipline and restraint only patience can produce. The ability to pause, breathe, assess, and choose the right response has saved lives, sometimes literally. Across my service in corrections, probation, law enforcement, crime prevention, and community relations, my arrest numbers remained minimal. What truly defined my work was the ability to strengthen the community through service, resolve disturbances through steady presence, and build lasting trust through patience and meaningful relationships.

In higher education, patience is equally essential. Working with students, families, faculty, and community partners requires recognizing that growth is a process. Not every student develops at the same pace, which is why catalytic leadership is so important. Not every partnership forms overnight. Not every initiative gains momentum immediately. Patience allows leaders to coach, mentor, cultivate, and build trust with the people and communities they serve.

As a Credit Union Associate Board Member, patience is the foundation of wise governance. Strategic decisions require long-term thinking. Financial oversight requires careful study. Leadership transitions require stability. The best board members understand that patience is not delay, it is clarity.

I learned the value of clarity early in my academic journey. After getting off course in college and earning a 1.94 GPA, I made the decision to refocus, rebuild, and realign my priorities. Through discipline and persistence, I ultimately made the Dean's List and later earned my doctoral degree, a testament to resilience, strategic planning, and setting achievable goals.

In that same spirit of growth, I continued gaining reputable credentials in the credit union movement by challenging myself and successfully completing the Board Development Certification School Exam, becoming a Certified Credit Union Board Member. This accomplishment reinforced my commitment to governance excellence and lifelong learning.

As a councilman, I often draw encouragement as I recount how patience shaped me through injury, recovery, transition, and other leadership challenges. When things do not transpire as fast as I would like, I remind myself that greatness requires timing, discipline, and trust in the process.

Patience in leadership also means giving others grace. Whether interacting with young men looking for direction, community members seeking support, or teammates navigating life, patience helps create safe spaces for growth. My mentorship programs, youth outreach efforts, and community initiatives are rooted in giving people room to evolve without judgment.

Patience is active. Patience is powerful. It is what allows leaders to remain emotionally grounded while moving purposefully toward long-term goals. It teaches us that setbacks are not final, delays are not denials, and every season of waiting has a purpose when you stay committed.

Original Quote by Michael A. Cadore, Ed.D. Copyright © 2025

If you feel delayed, you're not denied. The waiting room is just a classroom where the Lord refines your discipline for the next assignment.

-Cadore's Magnus Nugget

## Reflection Questions:

1. Where in your life are you being asked to wait and to trust?
2. What can you learn during the waiting season that will strengthen you later?

3. How can patience help you lead with greater empathy and grace?

_____

_____

_____

_____

_____

_____

_____

_____

_____

_____

_____

_____

_____

_____

_____

_____

_____

_____

## Principle 3 – Professionalism

Professionalism is not a uniform, a title, or a moment. Professionalism is a standard. It is the way you carry your character into every room, whether anyone acknowledges it or not. Long before I represented Eastern Kentucky University, a professional football organization, a law enforcement agency, a college, a credit union board, or the residents of the City of Rockledge, I learned professionalism at home. My parents taught me that your name is your first résumé.

How you speak, how you listen, how you treat people, and how you show up become your signature long before you ever sign a contract. My father would often say, "Mind your mouth," meaning think before you speak. That wisdom still applies today; especially in maintaining a positive professional mindset.

Sometimes the most damaging conversations are the ones we have with ourselves. Negative internal dialogue, self-doubt, and dismissing our own abilities can undermine the very confidence professionalism requires. We must speak professionally, dress professionally, and refuse to let the opinions of others define our value. Impostor syndrome can be subtle, but it can also be deeply destructive if we allow it to take root.

Professionalism is the daily decision to lead yourself in thought, in word, and in presence.

In Titusville High School's championship environment, professionalism showed up in the little things. Being on time. Being coachable. Being accountable when you miss an assignment. Respecting your teammates and respecting the game. We did more than win. We modeled maturity. That environment shaped a mindset which followed me for the rest of my life: *act like a professional long before you are paid like one.*

Even during the seasons when I sat on the bench with my teammate Darryll Gaymon, both of us playing behind two All-Americans, we remained prepared. We knew our time would come. During games, we kept the energy high by joking with each other, saying, "You brought the coffee, I brought the doughnuts." It was our way of staying ready, staying positive, and staying locked in. We waited patiently for our opportunity and when our number was called, we excelled.

At Eastern Kentucky University, professionalism deepened. College athletics force you to grow up quickly. Expectations rise. Responsibilities increase. Your margin for error decreases. I learned to balance academics, athletics, community expectations, and personal discipline. Every meeting, every practice, every weight-room session required showing up prepared physically, mentally, and emotionally. Professionalism is showing consistency even when no one applauds it.

Being drafted by the New Orleans Saints strengthened my understanding of professionalism. The NFL (National Football League) is a world where details matter. The standard is excellence. The mindset is competitive growth. Even though injury altered my path, the experience taught me the importance of preparation, communication, and accountability at the highest level. Competing in the World League with the Montreal Machine reinforced that same mindset. You represent not just yourself, but your team, your city, your family, and the people who believe in you.

When my journey transitioned into law enforcement, professionalism became even more essential. In this field, professionalism is measured not by titles, but by temperament. Your ability to de-escalate conflict, communicate clearly, and treat every community member with dignity becomes a daily test of character. You are expected to perform under pressure, make decisions with integrity, and uphold standards even when situations are complicated or charged with emotion. Professionalism in law enforcement is service with discipline, empathy, and respect.

My work at Eastern Florida State College continued to shape my understanding of professionalism in a new environment, education and community engagement. In higher education, professionalism means representing the college well, treating every student and family with dignity, and building relationships in the community on the foundation of transparency, trust, and commitment. Emails, meetings, partnerships, and programs all become reflections of how seriously you take your mission. You must know the mission, understand your role, and execute it with excellence.

As an Associate Board Member for Launch Credit Union, professionalism expanded again. In governance, professionalism means preparation, studying policies, reading financials, understanding compliance, asking informed questions, and maintaining confidentiality. It means respecting diverse viewpoints, working collaboratively with experienced board members, and contributing with humility, not ego. Governance requires maturity, foresight, and the willingness to serve as a steward rather than a spotlight-seeker.

As a city councilman, professionalism guides my service and is evidenced by honoring people, respecting processes, and showing up with consistency, for each resident, regardless of their stage of life, with genuine interest in their well-being.

Professionalism is also personal. It is how you treat your family. How you communicate with people who disagree with you. How you carry yourself on good days and how you stabilize yourself on challenging ones. Professionalism means choosing discipline over impulse and integrity over convenience. It means your word matters and your actions match your principles.

Every young person I mentor hears me say: "Professionalism is who you are when nobody is watching, and especially when everybody is watching." Whether speaking to youth, meeting with executives, mentoring young men, standing before students, or sitting in a boardroom, professionalism is your leadership signature.

Original Quote by Michael A. Cadore, Ed.D. Copyright © 2025

Excellence isn't about the suit or the badge; it's the quiet integrity you keep when no one, but your Creator, is watching.

-Cadore's Magnus Nugget

## Reflection Questions:

1. How do you demonstrate professionalism in everyday interactions?
2. What personal standard separates you from mediocrity?
3. How can professionalism inspire trust in those you lead?

_____

_____

_____

_____

_____

_____

_____

_____

_____

_____

_____

_____

## Principle 4 – Pride

Pride, when rooted in humility and responsibility, is one of the most powerful forces in leadership. It is not arrogance. It is not ego. It is not the desire for applause. True pride is the deep, steady awareness that your life, your name, and your choices carry weight. It is honoring where you come from, who poured into you, and the standard you represent.

I learned early that the Cadore name carried expectations. My father, Anthony V. Cadore Sr., carried himself with respect, dignity, discipline, and strength. My mother reinforced the values that shaped my foundation: faith, respect, accountability, and the belief that your actions should make your family proud. In our home, pride was not something spoken; it was something lived.

I never had the blessing of meeting my grandparents, but the qualities instilled in my father transcended to me and my brothers. Their legacy lived through him, and through him, it lives in us. I often wish I had the opportunity to tell my grandparents how proud I am of them and how deeply their strength continues to guide our family today.

At the age of 12, my mother reluctantly allowed me to play football. I remember her asking, "Do you know why you play so well?" I told her, "Because I can run very fast." She smiled and said, "Son, that is true. But God has blessed you with the ability not only to play this game but to play it well."

As the spiritual foundation of our home, my mother gave me one instruction that stayed with me for life: "Every time you score a touchdown, take a knee and give God thanks." That simple act became my earliest expression of praise; a reminder that success is a gift, not a guarantee. I honored my mother's request every time I scored, from Little League through college. While I never scored a touchdown professionally, I continue to honor our Heavenly Father every moment of every day carrying forward a legacy of faith, humility, gratitude, and purpose.

Though I was a sickly child, my mother never allowed me to speak about illness over my own life. She often said that seeing what God had done for me was the reason she gave her life to Christ. In her eyes, I was her miracle baby; her living testimony of grace, strength, and prayer.

Titusville High School further strengthened my foundation. Being part of a championship football program meant that pride was reflected in how you practiced, how you competed, and how you carried yourself in school and in the community. It meant understanding that your effort contributed to the legacy of those who came before you. Every time I lined up for a play, and every time I put on that jersey, I carried my family, my coaches, my teammates, and my community with me.

In 1988, I was honored to receive the Roy Kidd Award of Excellence, presented by The Worn Cleat Club. This recognition carried deep meaning not only because it bore the name of Coach Roy Kidd, a legendary figure at Eastern Kentucky University, but because of the values it represented.

The award was given "as a matter of pride," acknowledging respect, character, effort, and the way a young man carried himself on and off the field. To receive an honor rooted in respect for the man and his accomplishments was both humbling and affirming.

Coach Roy Kidd built more than football teams he built men. His standard of preparation, discipline, and accountability shaped my mindset as an athlete and later as a leader. Receiving this award from an organization tied to the history and brotherhood of EKU Football remains one of my most meaningful recognitions. It is a reminder that excellence is not measured only in stats or highlights. Excellence is measured in character, consistency, and how well you honor those who came before you.

At Eastern Kentucky University, pride took on new meaning. EKU wasn't just another program; it was a standard. Being part of a storied football tradition meant earning your place every day. Setting the kickoff-return record and being named All-Conference were honors, but what mattered most was knowing I represented my family, my school, and myself with integrity. Pride is not only found in achievements. Pride is reflected in the attitude, discipline, and consistency behind them. As we often said, "EKU is a matter of pride."

Being drafted by the New Orleans Saints brought another level of pride. It validated years of work, sacrifice, and preparation. Even though injury shifted my path, I never lost pride in the effort it took to get there. Competing for the Montreal Machine in the WLAF (World League of American Football) and finishing second in kickoff-return average affirmed a powerful truth: setbacks don't diminish pride; how you respond to them defines it.

Pride followed me into public safety, where service required courage, compassion, and character. I wore the badge with the same sense of responsibility I had carried on the field. Pride meant treating every community member with dignity and walking into every situation determined to leave people better than I found them. Professional pride is the backbone of effective policing and community trust.

In higher education at Eastern Florida State College, pride became purpose. Serving students, supporting families, building partnerships, and representing the college across Brevard County required consistency and credibility. Pride means ensuring every conversation, every program, and every interaction reflects excellence as a leader, as a father, as a mentor, and as a public servant.

As an Associate Board Member with Launch Credit Union, pride aligns with stewardship. Governance is not about recognition; it is about service. Pride is shown in preparation, participation, respect for diverse viewpoints, and making decisions that protect the financial well-being of members.

Pride is knowing you are contributing to something that strengthens the community. I appreciate the opportunity to represent a diverse group of people as a city councilman. I carry pride in my Grenadian heritage, my Titusville roots, and the Cadore name.

Pride is not arrogance. Pride is stewardship, honor, and legacy.

But pride is also personal. I take pride in my marriage to my Queen, Cornelia. Pride in my children: Princess Courtney, Princess Cierra, and Sir Michael II. Pride in the generations before me and the generations coming after me. Pride in the young men and women I mentor who courageously choose growth over excuses. Pride in every community program, every outreach event, and every life touched.

The right kind of pride elevates your posture, strengthens your decisions, and stabilizes your leadership. It reminds you that you represent more than yourself. It anchors you in purpose and pushes you to raise others as you rise.

Original Quote by Michael A. Cadore, Ed.D. Copyright © 2025

Take pride not in what you accomplished, but in the family name and community you honored by doing your absolute best today.

-Cadore's Magnus Nugget

31

# Reflection Questions:

1. How do you show pride in your work and community?
2. What does pride in your name and legacy mean to you?
3. How can pride become a tool for excellence rather than ego?

_____

_____

_____

_____

_____

_____

_____

_____

_____

_____

_____

_____

_____

_____

## Principle 5 – Persistence

Persistence is the engine behind every breakthrough. It is the willingness to continue when motivation fades, when circumstances shift, and when life hands you a challenge that tests your resolve. Persistence is not simply holding on; it is growing stronger while you hold on.

Persistence is developed long before victories. People often see the championship banners, the touchdowns, and the highlight moments, but they rarely see the early mornings, the conditioning drills, and the days when your body aches and your mind want to quit. My persistence was built on the hot fields of Titusville High School. It was built on summer workouts and late-night film sessions. It was built by learning to compete with heart, not entitlement.

I am thankful for the leadership and mentorship of my brothers: Jeff, Gary, Tony, and Joseph and the many athletes who would return home during the summers to train with us and show us what the next level demanded. Quitting wasn't an option; getting better through preparation was the expectation.

At Eastern Kentucky University, persistence became the difference between potential and performance. College athletics demanded more than talent. It required discipline through injury, consistency through competition, and humility through growth. When I set the 232-yard kickoff-return record against Louisiana-Monroe, it wasn't because of one play; it was the result of years of preparation and persistence working together.

Persistence showed its true power during my transition to professional football. Being drafted by the New Orleans Saints was an honor, but it was also the product of intentional preparation. For years, I woke up at 4:40 a.m. as a symbol of a personal standard; mind, body, and spirit aligned for excellence. If I could run 40 yards faster than 4.4 seconds, I believed I would get drafted. I ran a 4.36.

That number also reminded me of a foundational truth found in Mark 4:40, faith matters, "But He said to them, "Why are you so fearful? How *is it* that you have no faith?" To be persistent, you must believe.

Though an injury with the New Orleans Saints forced me into a season of waiting and recovery, I reflected on the fact that, physically, I was never "supposed" to play football at any level. My size, my childhood health challenges, and the odds were against me. That moment could have ended my journey. Many players never return from that kind of setback. But persistence wouldn't let me accept defeat. I committed myself to healing, rebuilding, training, and staying mentally sharp. That persistence led me to the World League of American Football, where I competed with the Montreal Machine and finished second in the league in kickoff-return average.

Persistence is not just for athletes; it is for leaders. When I entered law enforcement, persistence meant staying committed to excellence even on difficult days. It meant pushing through fatigue, navigating challenging situations, and earning community trust one interaction at a time. Persistence meant showing up for people who needed not just enforcement, but compassion, patience, and stability.

In higher education at Eastern Florida State College, persistence took on a new meaning. Building programs, establishing community partnerships, mentoring students, and supporting families all require unwavering commitment. Growth takes time. Momentum takes time. Trust takes time. Persistence is believing in the work before the results are visible.

As a Launch Credit Union Associate Board Member, persistence is essential to governance. Organizational success does not happen overnight. It requires long-term thinking, data-driven decisions, and consistent engagement. Persistence is showing up to every meeting prepared. Reading every packet, asking thoughtful questions, and staying focused on the long-term financial health of the members you serve.

As a city councilman, I prioritize the generational advancement of my community, through stability and innovation. Being persistence over time, has taught me to remain faithful to the mission even when the outcome is uncertain and in spite of contrary opinions.

Persistence also shows up in my personal life:

- ❖ Marriage requires persistence; showing up for your partner, communicating with love, and choosing unity even when life gets challenging.
- ❖ Fatherhood requires persistence; pouring into your children, guiding them, supporting their dreams, and being the example they watch.
- ❖ Persistence is spiritual, emotional, mental, and physical.
- ❖ It is choosing growth when comfort is easier.
- ❖ It is believing in yourself when obstacles arise.
- ❖ It is refusing to let temporary setbacks define your permanent identity.
- ❖ Persistence is the champion's mindset.
- ❖ Persistence is the servant leader's posture.
- ❖ Persistence is the Magnus way.
- ❖ Magnus #Greatness

Original Quote by Michael A. Cadore, Ed.D. Copyright © 2025

Pressure is the furnace that either breaks you or forges your purpose. Don't quit when you're seconds away from the breakthrough.

-Cadore's Magnus Nugget

## Reflection Questions:

1. When have you had to persist despite difficulty?
2. Who or what keeps you motivated when progress feels slow?
3. What vision are you willing to pursue even when others can't see it yet?

_____

_____

_____

_____

_____

_____

_____

_____

## Principle 6 – Praise

Praise is a form of leadership. It is the ability to recognize, uplift, encourage, and affirm the people around you. Praise is not flattery. It is not performance. It is intentional acknowledgment; an act of leadership that strengthens relationships, builds confidence, and inspires excellence. Leaders who praise others create cultures where people feel valued, seen, and motivated to grow.

I learned early in life that praise has power. Growing up in a home grounded in love and discipline, my parents taught us to give thanks no matter how big or small the blessing. Saying "thank you" to those who helped you is a sign of respect and humility. Not because my parents believed in making life easy, but because they believed in reinforcing the right behaviors and honoring the people who support you. Praise is a way of saying, "I see your effort. Keep going. And thank you for helping me."

At Titusville High School, praise was woven into the championship culture. Coaches praised effort, not just results. Teammates celebrated growth, not just touchdowns or big plays. Praise created unity. It created momentum. It helped us push through long practices, tough games, and high expectations. Positive reinforcement is a cornerstone of every high-performing team.

At Eastern Kentucky University, praise took on a more strategic and intentional form. Coaches praised resilience, discipline, and consistency, not just the final performance. It was about the preparation, the execution, and the character displayed in the moment. That kind of praise keeps leaders grounded and focused on what truly matters.

In professional football, praise is earned. Being drafted into the NFL, competing with the Montreal Machine, and fighting back from injuries required mental toughness. Teammates respected resilience. Coaches praised commitment. Praise is a way for teams to build trust; especially in a game where adversity is constant, and careers can change in an instant.

In law enforcement, praise plays an even more vital role. Work is demanding, the environment unpredictable, and the stakes high. A word of encouragement after a difficult call, acknowledgment of restraint in a tense situation, or appreciation for consistent professionalism can mean the difference between burnout and renewed purpose. Praise helps maintain morale and emotional stability in a field where stress can erode both over time.

At Eastern Florida State College, praise is a leadership tool I use often. Students flourish when they are affirmed. Staff members stay motivated when they feel valued. Community partners remain engaged when their contributions are recognized. Praise builds relationships and reminds people that their efforts matter. They are seen, appreciated, and essential to the mission.

As an Associate Board Member at Launch Credit Union, I witness firsthand how praise strengthens governance. Boardrooms perform better when members feel respected and acknowledged. Praise enhances collaboration, encourages diverse perspectives, and builds trust. Recognizing the work of others, whether senior board members, executives, or staff reinforces a culture of mutual respect and shared purpose.

There is a saying, "The squeaky wheel gets the oil." I have found this to be true serving on the city council as I interact with the public. Knowing that praise shifts mindsets and turns adversity into gratitude; I often utilize this practical principle to navigate, mediate, and resolve conflicts. Shaped by mother's prayers and my family's faith, praise is the fuel that strengthens leaders.

Praise also belongs at home. My Queen, Cornelia, and our children are constants in my life. Celebrating their victories, big or small, reinforces love, unity, and gratitude. Praise builds stronger families. It builds stronger marriages. It strengthens the bonds that sustain leaders through every season of life. We must be mindful that it does no good to be "Employee of the Month" or "Employee of the Year" if we are not present and accessible to our family. Too often, goals are achieved but never celebrated properly because we were not there with the people who matter most.

As a mentor, I have seen how praise can transform the trajectory of young people. Many youth rarely hear consistent positive reinforcement. A simple, sincere word of affirmation can ignite confidence, reduce self-doubt, and open the door to new possibilities. Praise can be the spark that awakens potential.

Leaders who praise intentionally create environments where people give their best. Not out of fear, but out of pride. Praise builds loyalty, trust, and connection. It strengthens teams, organizations, and communities.

Stop waiting for the harvest to thank the farmer. A grateful leader is an anchored leader; praise uplifts the entire mission.

-Cadore's Magnus Nugget

## Reflection Questions:

1. Who do you need to thank today for helping you on your journey?
2. How often do you celebrate small wins with your team or family?
3. How can gratitude help you lead with joy and humility?

_____

_____

_____

_____

_____

_____

_____

## Principle 7 – Paramount

Paramount means "above all." It is the principle that clarifies your priorities, shapes your identity, and anchors your decisions. What is paramount in your life will always reveal itself. Not through your words, but through your habits, your commitments, and your consistency. Leadership is not simply what you do. Leadership is what you value, protect, and elevate.

For me, service has always been paramount. Long before titles, trophies, or positions, service was the heartbeat of my purpose. I wanted to be on the team, have a sense of belonging, carry my own weight, and help others. I watched my parents demonstrate service with humility by helping neighbors, showing kindness, and giving without expecting anything in return. They didn't talk about service. They lived it. Their example became the blueprint for every phase of my leadership.

Early on, I learned what community truly meant. Titusville High School embraced me, challenged me, and helped shape my path. On the football field, service meant being accountable to my teammates. In the classroom, service meant respecting teachers and peers. In the community, service meant representing not just myself, but everyone who believed in me.

These experiences taught me that leadership must extend beyond personal success. That is why my ethos was born, *"If you don't serve your community now, don't expect your community to serve you later."*

At Eastern Kentucky University, what was paramount became even clearer. Yes, football was important. Yes, academics mattered. But what stood above everything was character. Coaches reminded us constantly that championships fade, but character remains. Being All-Conference, breaking records, and representing EKU were blessings but none of it held value without integrity. Character was paramount. I never wanted to bring disrespect to anything or anyone.

When I entered professional football, the stakes grew higher. Training camps, playbooks, competition, injuries, and opportunities all competed for mental space. I learned quickly that emotional maturity was paramount. The NFL tests more than your body. It tests your mindset. My injury didn't just challenge my career; it clarified my priorities. It reminded me that purpose must be bigger than position.

Playing in the World League of American Football with the Montreal Machine reinforced what was paramount: resilience, gratitude, and discipline. Competing at that level requires keeping first things first:

health, consistency, attitude, and teamwork. You cannot lead in chaos if you do not know what matters most.

When my journey led me into public safety, "paramount" took on its deepest meaning. In this field, lives are at stake. Emotions run high. Every response has consequences. *What was paramount?* Safety. Integrity. Respect. Compassion. Public trust. I learned that executing your duties without losing your humanity is the true measure of a public servant.

At Eastern Florida State College, service became paramount on an even larger scale. Students, families, seniors, veterans, staff, and community partners need leadership who are engaged, responsive, and present. Programs must be built. Partnerships must be nurtured. Outreach must be sustained. Showing up consistently, especially when people need you most is paramount to my role, my mission, and the college's mission.

As an Associate Board Member at Launch Credit Union, stewardship is paramount. Governance isn't about accolades it is about responsibility. Protecting member interests, strengthening financial wellness, asking informed questions, and supporting the executive team require clarity of priorities. Transparency is paramount. Accountability is paramount. Ethical leadership is paramount.

My family, my faith, my integrity, and my service are paramount as I make decisions and prioritize initiatives as a part of the city council, knowing that my actions have direct results in my community, therefore my household.

In my personal life, my faith and my family remain paramount. My Queen, Cornelia, and our children are the foundation of my "why." They remind me daily that leadership starts at home. Being present, loving, supportive, consistent, and committed is paramount in fatherhood and marriage.

When your priorities are clear, your decisions become easier. When what is paramount truly sits at the top, distractions lose their power. Leaders who lack clarity chase everything. Leaders who know what is paramount chase purpose.

Original Quote by Michael A. Cadore, Ed.D. Copyright © 2025

Your purpose must be paramount, because when the title is gone, your 'why' is the only thing left to build the legacy.

-Cadore's Magnus Nugget

## Reflection Questions:

1. What is truly paramount in your life right now?
2. How do you align your decisions with your purpose?
3. Who benefits from the work you do daily?

_____

_____

_____

_____

_____

_____

_____

_____

_____

_____

_____

_____

## Principle 8 – Respect

Respect is the foundation of every meaningful relationship, every successful team, and every effective leader. It is the one principle that transcends age, background, profession, and title. Respect is the universal language of leadership. It is how you honor others, honor yourself, and honor the responsibilities placed in your hands.

I learned respect early. Growing up in a home where discipline and dignity were non-negotiable, my parents taught me that respect was shown through your tone, your posture, your work ethic, and your treatment of others. Respect was essential in the way we spoke to adults, the way we treated our neighbors, and the way we carried the Cadore name. Respect was not something demanded, it was something demonstrated.

We had to carry ourselves with respect, humility, and gratitude. If not, there were dire consequences and discipline. In return, I learned to respect the people, traditions, and standards that shaped the city. On the football field, respect meant treating your teammates like brothers, respecting your coaches' guidance, and respecting the championship culture that existed long before you arrived.

At Eastern Kentucky University, respect became the heartbeat of team culture. Respect for the process. Respect for competition. Respect for the game. Respect for the weight room, the classroom, the university, and the opportunity. Coaches and team-mates taught me that you cannot lead people you do not respect, and you cannot earn respect without giving it first.

Professional football reinforced this truth. Competing in the WLAF with the Montreal Machine required respecting the grind, the speed of the game, and the diversity of teammates from different countries and backgrounds. Respect was not just a principle it was a necessity. Without respect, teams fall apart. With respect, they trust each other enough to excel.

In law enforcement, respect becomes even more critical. Every call, every encounter, every moment of tension tests your ability to respect human dignity. Respect in policing is listening before reacting. It is treating people with fairness even when emotions run high. It is honoring the badge by remembering that authority is not entitlement, it is responsibility. Respect builds trust, and trust strengthens communities.

At Eastern Florida State College, respect shapes every interaction with students seeking direction, parents seeking clarity, faculty seeking support, and community partners seeking collaboration. Respect creates access. It opens doors. It builds partnerships that last. When you treat people with respect, you empower them to rise.

As an Associate Board Member at Launch Credit Union, respect is essential for governance. Respecting diverse viewpoints leads to stronger decisions. Respecting the institution's mission ensures every vote and every recommendation protects the financial well-being of the members. Respect means speaking with honesty, listening with humility, and leading with integrity.

Being the voice of my community, as a councilman, I prioritize respect. It is a foundational requirement collectively in leadership, family, and community, to ensure clear communication and thorough consideration of diverse viewpoints.

Respect also defines a leader's personal life. Respecting your spouse, your children, your elders, and your friends creates stability. My Queen, Cornelia, and our children have always been central to my leadership journey. Respecting them means valuing time, communication, unity, and love.

Respect extends to mentorship as well. When I mentor young men, I respect their stories, their struggles, and their potential. Respect allows me to speak life into them without judgment. It helps them trust me enough to grow. Many young people today have never experienced consistent respect. When you show others respect, you unlock the leader within them.

Ultimately, respect is a mirror. It reflects your character. It shapes your reputation. It determines how people experience your leadership. You cannot demand what you do not demonstrate. Leaders who respect others become leaders worth following.

Original Quote by Michael A. Cadore, Ed.D. Copyright © 2025

Talent might get you the meeting, but respect is the currency that keeps you at the table, especially with those who challenge you.

-Cadore's Magnus Nugget

# Reflection Questions:

1. How do you show respect to people who challenge you?
2. What habits demonstrate respect for yourself and others?
3. How can respect help heal the divisions in your community or workplace?

_____

_____

_____

_____

_____

_____

_____

_____

_____

_____

_____

_____

_____

_____

## Principle 9 – Reflection

Reflection is a leadership superpower. It is the ability to pause, look inward, evaluate your choices, and grow from every experience, both good and difficult. Leaders who reflect evolve. Leaders who refuse to reflect are in jeopardy of becoming obsolete. Reflection turns moments into wisdom, challenges into lessons, and successes into strategies for the future.

I learned the value of reflection early in life. Growing up, my parents encouraged me to slow down, think before reacting, and look for deeper meaning in everything I experienced. Whether it involved school, sports, or everyday decisions, they wanted me to understand not just what happened, but what I could learn from it. That became the foundation of my leadership mindset.

During my time at Titusville High School, reflection happened after practice, after games, and after difficult conversations with coaches or teammates. Championship teams don't just work hard, they reflect hard. We studied film, analyzed mistakes, identified strengths, and evaluated opportunities. Reflection sharpened my discipline and helped me mature as a young man navigating expectations, adversity, and identity.

I remember Coach Al Werneke once telling us we would be lucky to win three games after our first state championship because we had lost so much talent. We could have accepted that but instead, we reflected, grew, and showed him and our community that we were champions in more ways than one.

At Eastern Kentucky University, reflection became even more intentional. After games, I watched film not to celebrate highlights, but to examine movement, posture, decision-making, timing, and opportunities for improvement. Reflection helped me break records because it forced me to study the details. Champions are not defined by one performance. They are defined by how they evaluate themselves after each one.

Reflection became even more critical during my transition to professional football. Being drafted by the New Orleans Saints was a dream realized, but injury forced me into the deep end of reflection. I had to sit with questions: *Who am I without football? How do I rebuild? What is God trying to show me?* Those reflective moments shaped the leader I became, long before I put on a uniform again in the World League of American Football. I had to confront the truth that I was never "supposed" to play organized football at all and yet, by God's grace, I did.

In the WLAF with the Montreal Machine, reflection continued to guide me. Every kickoff return, every practice, every opportunity was a chance to learn. Reflection helped me push through doubt, refine my technique, and finish second in the entire league in kickoff-return average. It wasn't just talent it was reflection that kept me evolving.

In public safety, reflection was essential. In a field where every encounter can impact a life, reflection kept me grounded, emotionally stable, and committed to serving with integrity. It allowed me to evaluate not just what happened, but how I handled it, and how I could improve the next time. Reflection made me a protector, not just an officer.

"Treat others how you wish to be treated" wasn't just a phrase it was a core value. My father served as a civilian police officer for 27 years and earned tremendous respect. My oldest brother also served in public safety as a probation officer. I was destined to serve, too. Reflection kept my service sincere.

At Eastern Florida State College, reflection became part of my daily leadership rhythm. After events, community meetings, student interactions, or team discussions, I reflect: *What went well? Where can we improve? Who was impacted? How can we serve better?* Reflection fuels innovation, strengthens relationships, and builds trust.

As an Associate Board Member at Launch Credit Union, reflection supports wise governance. Reviewing reports, policies, financials, and outcomes requires thoughtful analysis. Reflection allows board members to make decisions based on clarity, not impulse. On purpose, not pressure. Governance without reflection becomes reactionary, not strategic.

When addressing residential, commercial, and recreational community concerns, as a councilman, reflection gives clarity. Collectively, it allows us to see progress, learn from mistakes, and stay grounded in purpose, not ever-changing opinions.

Reflection also shapes my personal life. In marriage, reflection helps me become a better husband. More patient, more attentive, and more supportive. As a father, it helps me understand how to guide my children through their own journeys. As a community servant, reflection helps me give my best to the people I lead, love, and represent.

True reflection requires honesty. You must face your strengths, your weaknesses, your wins, your losses, and your blind spots. Reflection is not self-criticism.

Reflection is self-awareness. Leaders who reflect grow. Leaders who avoid reflection remain stuck.

Original Quote by Michael A. Cadore, Ed.D. Copyright © 2025

If you refuse to pause, you refuse to grow. Wisdom is what you pull out of the quiet mirror of reflection, not what you skim off the noise.

-Cadore's Magnus Nugget

# Reflection Questions:

1. How often do you pause to evaluate your leadership or personal journey?
2. What recent lesson changed your perspective?
3. Who in your life helps you stay accountable to your growth?

_____

_____

_____

_____

_____

## Principle 10 – Raise

Raise is the principle of elevation: lifting yourself, lifting others, and lifting the standard in every environment you touch. To raise means to build, to grow, to strengthen, and to leave things better than you find them. Raise is the Magnus commitment to continuous improvement, legacy building, and generational impact.

I learned the importance of raising the standard early. In my home, respect and hard work weren't demanded; they were expected. My parents believed that if you carry the Cadore name, you must lift others through your effort, your attitude, and your example. That mindset prepared me for every arena I would one day enter: athletics, law enforcement, higher education, community leadership, and board governance.

While in Titusville High School, raising the standard became a way of life. Football was never just about winning games it was about raising young men into leaders. Each practice challenged us to raise our performance. Each game pushed us to raise our competitiveness. Each teammate inspired us to raise our discipline. Championship cultures do not happen by accident. They happen when everyone commits to raising the standard daily.

At Eastern Kentucky University, raising the standard meant stepping into a program where tradition mattered. EKU was built on legacy championships, excellence, and pride. Becoming All-Conference and setting the kickoff-return record required more than talent. It required raising my preparation, my focus, and my commitment beyond what I believed was possible. When you raise your standard, you often unlock abilities you never knew you had.

In professional football, raising the standard became survival. Competing in the WLAF with the Montreal Machine required raising my intensity, raising my conditioning, raising my mental sharpness, and raising my leadership. Finishing second in the league in kickoff-return average was not just a statistic, it was proof of raising the standard in spite of adversity. Injuries tried to break me. Persistence raised me.

When I entered public safety, raising the standard meant serving with integrity, compassion, and courage every single day. The profession tests your patience, your emotions, and your resilience. Raising the standard in policing meant refusing to cut corners, refusing to compromise dignity, and refusing to let the job harden your heart. My goal was to raise professionalism, raise community trust, and raise expectations of what service should look like.

At Eastern Florida State College, raising the standard became my leadership mandate. Whether supporting students, collaborating with faculty, hosting community events, or building partnerships across Brevard County, the mission was always the same: raise opportunities, raise engagement, excellence, and raise impact. Leadership in education is not about titles. It is about transforming lives. To do that, you must raise the bar every day.

As an Associate Board Member at Launch Credit Union, raising the standard means contributing fresh ideas, asking thoughtful questions, and helping build a stronger future for members. Raising the standard in governance requires financial literacy, strategic thinking, integrity, and collaboration. Board service is not ceremonial it becomes transformational when leaders commit to raising expectations.

Serving on Rockledge City Council, restoring the Student Advisory Council, supporting Aging Matters, coordinating food drives, and running unopposed for two terms reflected the trust placed in leadership that lifts the community. Raise means elevation—raising your standards, raising your community, raising your family. It means investing in the next generation and lifting those around you.

In my personal life, raising the standard is about legacy. For my Queen, Cornelia, and our children, I strive to model what love, unity, discipline, and leadership look like. I want them to inherit not just my successes, but my standards. Parenting is leadership. Marriage is leadership. Raising your family requires raising yourself.

Raising the standard also extends to the community. Whether mentoring youth, speaking to students, guiding young men, or partnering with local organizations, I believe that leaders must raise the next generation. If we do not lift our youth, we leave them vulnerable to the pressures and pitfalls of this world. Raising others is the purest form of service.

Raise means growth. Raise means elevation. Raise means refusing to remain the same. It means reaching higher while pulling others with you. Leaders who raise the standard leave legacies that outlive them.

Original Quote by Michael A. Cadore, Ed.D. Copyright © 2025

A ladder is only useful if someone else can climb it. Your true measure is the height of those you help lift.

-Cadore's Magnus Nugget

# Reflection Questions:

1. Who has helped raise you into the leader you are today?
2. Who are you intentionally raising right now?
3. How can your daily actions build a legacy that outlives you?

_____

_____

_____

_____

_____

_____

_____

_____

_____

_____

_____

# Part II:
# Building a Magnus Mindset

## Magnus Nuggets of Leadership

Remember, Magnus Nuggets are designed to educate, encourage, and empower you through the journey of leadership.

Below is a list of additional Magnus Nuggets. Write one Magnus Nugget at the top of your planner or calendar each week. Let it set your tone, focus, and mindset. Use them as daily affirmations, journal prompts, or group discussion starters:

❖ "Service is the rent we pay for the privilege of living in our community."

❖ "Greatness isn't about recognition; it's about responsibility."

❖ "Leadership without love is direction without connection."

❖ "Your influence begins where your ego ends."

❖ "The power to serve is the power to transform."

## Legacy Notes

In this section, please take a moment to reflect on the legacy you're building. Leadership is temporary, but legacy is timeless.

Use the prompts below to write your reflections in the space provided or create your own "Legacy Letter" to your future self or to the next generation of leaders who will follow you.

# Legacy Reflection Prompts:

1. What values do you want to pass down to your children, students, or team?
2. How do you want people to describe your leadership when you're not in the room?
3. What will your community remember you for twenty years from now?

_____

_____

_____

_____

_____

_____

_____

_____

_____

## Vision Planner: Your 10-Year Impact

Use this section to map out your leadership vision and goals.

**Step 1:** Identify Your Vision Statement

Write one clear sentence that defines your long-term leadership goal.

Example: "To educate, equip, and empower communities through servant leadership."

_____

_____

_____

_____

_____

_____

**Step 2:** Set Your 3 Pillars of Focus
  ❖ Personal Development
  ❖ Professional Growth
  ❖ Community Impact

_____

_____

_____

_____

_____

_____

_____

_____

_____

_____

_____

_____

_____

_____

_____

_____

_____

**Step 3:** Action Steps

List 3 practical actions you can take this year to advance each pillar.

❖ Personal
❖ Professional
❖ Community

_____

_____

_____

_____

_____

_____

_____

_____

_____

_____

_____

_____

_____

_____

_____

**Step 4:** Accountability Partners

Who will hold you accountable and support your growth? Write their names and roles.

_____

_____

_____

_____

_____

_____

_____

_____

**Inspirational Quotes:**

Continually, use these quotes to refresh your mind and spirit when the journey gets tough. Visit this section to intentionally meditate on one quote at a time, as it pertains to the area of encouragement you are seeking. Write down what it means to you:

❖ "Leadership is not about asserting power or being in charge, it's about serving others and taking care of those in your charge."

– Simon Sinek[1]

_____

_____

_____

_____

_____

_____

❖ "For as the body without the spirit is dead, so faith without works is dead also."

– James 2:26

_____

_____

_____

_____

_____

_____

_____

❖ "If serving is beneath you, then leadership is beyond you."

– Bishop Dale Bronner[2]

_____

_____

_____

_____

_____

_____

_____

❖ "You can't lead people you don't love."

– Dr. Michael A. Cadore Sr.

_____

_____

_____

_____

_____

_____

_____

❖ "Your presence should make others better, not bitter."
- Magnus Solutions

_____

_____

_____

_____

_____

_____

❖ "Character is built when no one is watching but God."

_____

_____

_____

_____

_____

❖ "Gratitude turns routine into worship."

_____

_____

_____

_____

_____

❖ "Vision without values is vanity."

_____

_____

_____

_____

_____

❖ "You can't mentor what you won't model."

_____

_____

_____

_____

_____

❖ Excellence is a choice repeated daily. "We are what we repeatedly do. Excellence, then, is not an act, but a habit."

– Aristotle[3]

_____

_____

_____

_____

_____

❖ "The true test of leadership is what happens after you leave the room."

_____

_____

_____

_____

_____

_____

❖ "Faith fuels focus."

_____

_____

_____

_____

_____

❖ "Humility is strength under control."

-Tim Kight[4]

_____

_____

_____

_____

_____

_____

❖ "Community is the classroom where leadership is tested."

_____

_____

_____

_____

_____

_____

❖ "Consistency creates credibility."[5]

_____

_____

_____

_____

_____

_____

❖ "Patience is the bridge between purpose and promise."

_____

_____

_____

_____

_____

_____

❖ "Discipline is doing what's right even when it's inconvenient."

_____

_____

_____

_____

_____

_____

❖ "Legacy is built through everyday choices."[6]

_____

_____

_____

_____

_____

❖ "The loudest leaders are not always the most effective. Quiet consistency wins."[7]

_____

_____

_____

_____

_____

❖ "Gratitude is the language of true greatness."

_____

_____

_____

_____

_____

_____

❖ "A servant heart turns power into purpose."

_____

_____

_____

_____

_____

❖ Write a few of your own favorite quotes below to keep your motivation personal and powerful.

_____

_____

_____

_____

_____

_____

[1] Art. "Connect Global." Connect Global, 17 Aug. 2023, connectglobal.org/articles/leadership-the-art-of-caring-for-those-in-your-charge.

[2] Reuter, Mike. "If Serving Is below You, Leadership Is beyond You." Three Minute Leadership, 17 May 2020, threeminuteleadership.com/2020/05/17/if-serving-is-below-you-leadership-is-beyond-you/.

[3] L, Kenneth. "Aristotle Quote about Excellence. We Are What We Repeatedly Do... Meaning." TOKI Motivation, 24 June 2025, tokimotivation.com/quote-meanings/aristotle-quote-about-excellence-we-are-what-we-repeatedly-do-excellence-habit/. Accessed 10 Dec. 2025.

[4] "Strength under Control." Acalltoexcellence.com, 7 Dec. 2020, acalltoexcellence.com/strength-under-control/. Accessed 10 Dec. 2025.

[5] "Consistency: Trust and Consistency: The Importance of Reliable Leadership." FasterCapital, fastercapital.com/content/Consistency--Trust-and-Consistency--The-Importance-of-Reliable-Leadership.html.

[6] Simpson, DW. "Build Your Legacy and Leave a Lasting Impact - DW Simpson." DW Simpson, 17 July 2024, www.dwsimpson.com/2024/07/17/build-your-legacy-and-leave-a-lasting-impact/.

[7] Fabio Caipirinha. "Quiet Leadership: The Power of Leading without Raising Your Voice." Substack.com, Fabio Caipirinha's Substack, 21 Feb. 2025, fabiocaipirinha.substack.com/p/quiet-leadership-the-power-of-leading. Accessed 10 Dec. 2025.

## Closing Summary (The Magnus Mindset)

Leadership is not a destination; it's a daily decision. Each morning, we rise with the opportunity to serve, to grow, and to give.

The Magnus Leadership Principles of Success are not just philosophies. They are practices that transform how we live, love, and lead.

If you've made it to this point in the book, pause and celebrate your growth. You've reflected, planned, and made space for purpose. Now it's time to apply it. Greatness does not wait for convenience. Greatness responds to conviction.

Take what you've learned and pour it into your home, your workplace, your school, your community. Someone is waiting for your leadership to unlock theirs.

The Magnus Mindset is simple yet powerful: Educate. Encourage. Empower.

When you embrace those three actions, you don't just lead, you transform. And always remember: *"If you don't serve your community now, don't expect your community to serve you later."*

## Commitment to Greatness Pledge

Read this pledge aloud. Share it with your family, team, or organization. Let it remind you of the responsibility that comes with influence.

- ❖ I pledge to lead with purpose, patience, and professionalism.
- ❖ I will take pride in my actions and persist through challenges.
- ❖ I will praise others, respect differences, and reflect often.
- ❖ I will keep what is paramount at the center of my decisions.
- ❖ I will raise others as I rise.
- ❖ I commit to living with excellence, integrity, and compassion, knowing that my leadership is not about power, but about service.

Signed,

_____ Date: _____

# Part III:
# Reflection & Engagement

## Magnus Moments

### 1: Preparation

*"Preparation is respecting the opportunity before it arrives.
When God opens a door,
your readiness determines whether you can walk through it."*

### Backstory:

As I previously shared with you, I learned preparation from my father, Anthony V. Cadore Sr. He taught us that your name is your first résumé and how you prepare shows God and your community that you honor the blessings coming your way.

Preparation is the quiet rehearsal for God's divine assignment. You don't earn the stage without putting in the time backstage.

### How will you apply this principle to your life?

_____

_____

## 2: Patience

*"Patience is trusting God's timing*
*more than your own pressure.*
*Growth doesn't rush.*
*Growth matures."*

### Backstory:

My mother taught me patience through faith. She prayed over us daily and always reminded me that delay is not denial, sometimes God is preparing you for what you cannot yet see.

Patience is proof that your faith is stronger than your impatience. Trust the process, because the process is preparing the leader.

### How will you apply this principle to your life?

_____

_____

_____

_____

_____

_____

_____

_____

_____

### 3: Professionalism

*"Professionalism is how you carry your character when no one is watching. Your name walks into the room before you do."*

### Backstory:

One of my dad's coined phrases, "Mind your mouth," taught me that how you speak, how you listen, and how you honor people is your first mark of professionalism, long before any title or promotion.

Professionalism *professes* your reputation, based on your words, actions, beliefs, and response to difficult situations.

### How will you apply this principle to your life?

_____

_____

_____

_____

_____

_____

_____

_____

_____

## 4: Pride

*"Pride is honoring the people
who poured into you: your family,
your mentors, and your community;
every time you step onto the field of life."*

### Backstory:

In every endeavor, personal or professional, I carry my community with me. It is not *only* about me. At all times, I represent my family, coaches, organizational affiliations, and everyone who believes in me.

### How will you apply this principle to your life?

_____

_____

_____

_____

_____

_____

_____

_____

_____

_____

_____

_____

_____

## 5: Persistence

*"Persistence is faith in motion.*
*It's what remains when the crowd*
*goes home and the odds say stop."*

### Backstory:

When I ran a 4.36 to earn my NFL opportunity, it wasn't talent alone. It was years of early mornings, setbacks, and determination to honor the gift God placed in me.

When you choose persistence as your posture, you turn every obstacle into an altar of learning and progress into your pattern.

### How will you apply this principle to your life?

_____

_____

_____

_____

_____

_____

_____

_____

_____

_____

## 6: Praise

*"Praise is a leader's reminder
that we didn't get here alone.
Gratitude keeps your heart lifted
and your purpose aligned."*

### Backstory:

Every touchdown from Little League through college, I took a knee because my mother told me, "Give God thanks." Praise became my posture long before leadership became my platform.

### How will you apply this principle to your life?

_____

_____

_____

_____

_____

_____

_____

_____

_____

_____

_____

_____

_____

## 7: Paramount

*"What is paramount in your life becomes the compass that guides your decisions. Keep God first, family close, and service at the center."*

### Backstory:

Coach Roy Kidd reminded us that football was what we did, not who we were. What matters most is faith, family, and character.

### How will you apply this principle to your life?

_____

_____

_____

_____

_____

_____

_____

_____

_____

_____

_____

_____

_____

## 8: Respect

*"Respect is earned through consistency,
strengthened through humility,
and sustained through service."*

### Backstory:

Growing up, respect wasn't optional. It was expected. From my home to the field, we learned to respect the people around us, the game, and ourselves.

I am beyond grateful to have been influenced by people who modeled mutual respect and never tolerated disrespect.

### How will you apply this principle to your life?

_____

_____

_____

_____

_____

_____

_____

_____

_____

_____

_____

_____

_____

## 9: Reflection

*"Reflection is where God reveals
the lessons success often hides.
Look back only to learn
then keep moving forward."*

### Backstory:

Reflection keeps me grounded. It reminds me that every experience, good or difficult, comes with a lesson meant to strengthen success.

Reflection is the essential work where a life of service is forged into a legacy of wisdom for the next generation of bridge-builders.

### How will you apply this principle to your life?

_____

_____

_____

_____

_____

_____

_____

_____

_____

_____

_____

_____

_____

_____

_____

_____

_____

_____

_____

_____

_____

_____

_____

_____

_____

_____

_____

_____

_____

_____

_____

_____

## 10: Raise

*"To raise others is to honor your purpose.
Greatness grows when you lift
the people around you."*

### Backstory:

From mentoring youth to serving on Rockledge City Council, raising others has always been my mission: If you don't serve your community now, don't expect your community to serve you later.

### How will you apply this principle to your life?

_____

_____

_____

_____

_____

_____

_____

_____

_____

_____

_____

_____

### Magnus Reflection Journal Pages

Leadership is not a destination; it's a daily decision. Each morning, we rise with the opportunity to serve, to grow, and to give.

Use these pages to record your lessons, dreams, and goals as you apply the Magnus Leadership Principles of Success. The purpose of this section is to review, record, and recognize your growth. Allow time to celebrate each accomplishment, while maximizing your forward momentum. Begin with the Magnus Reflection Prompts and complete a Journal Page during your scheduled time to reflect (daily, weekly, or monthly).

# Magnus Reflection Prompts:

1. How have you changed since beginning this book?
2. What action will you take this month to lead differently?
3. How can you use your influence to raise someone else?

_____

_____

_____

_____

## Journal Page

Date:_____

I learned that leadership is about _____

_____

My proudest leadership moment was _____

_____

My next step toward purpose is _____

_____

A challenge I faced recently taught me _____

_____

One Magnus Nugget that spoke to me is _____

_____

I am grateful for _____

_____

I will show gratitude by _____

_____

One person who I can serve better is _____

_____

**Journal Page**  Date:_____

I learned that leadership is about _____

_____

My proudest leadership moment was _____

_____

My next step toward purpose is _____

_____

A challenge I faced recently taught me _____

_____

One Magnus Nugget that spoke to me is _____

_____

I am grateful for _____

_____

I will show gratitude by _____

_____

One person who I can serve better is _____

_____

## Journal Page

Date:_____

I learned that leadership is about _____

_____

My proudest leadership moment was _____

_____

My next step toward purpose is _____

_____

A challenge I faced recently taught me _____

_____

One Magnus Nugget that spoke to me is _____

_____

I am grateful for _____

_____

I will show gratitude by _____

_____

One person who I can serve better is _____

_____

**Journal Page**  **Date:_____**

I learned that leadership is about _____

_____

My proudest leadership moment was _____

_____

My next step toward purpose is _____

_____

A challenge I faced recently taught me _____

_____

One Magnus Nugget that spoke to me is _____

_____

I am grateful for _____

_____

I will show gratitude by _____

_____

One person who I can serve better is _____

_____

**Journal Page**  **Date:**_____

I learned that leadership is about _____

_____

My proudest leadership moment was _____

_____

My next step toward purpose is _____

_____

A challenge I faced recently taught me _____

_____

One Magnus Nugget that spoke to me is _____

_____

I am grateful for _____

_____

I will show gratitude by _____

_____

One person who I can serve better is _____

_____

**Journal Page**  Date:_____

I learned that leadership is about _____

_____

My proudest leadership moment was _____

_____

My next step toward purpose is _____

_____

A challenge I faced recently taught me _____

_____

One Magnus Nugget that spoke to me is _____

_____

I am grateful for _____

_____

I will show gratitude by _____

_____

One person who I can serve better is _____

_____

*Journal Page*  Date:_____

I learned that leadership is about _____

_____

My proudest leadership moment was _____

_____

My next step toward purpose is _____

_____

A challenge I faced recently taught me _____

_____

One Magnus Nugget that spoke to me is _____

_____

I am grateful for _____

_____

I will show gratitude by _____

_____

One person who I can serve better is _____

_____

## Journal Page  Date:_____

I learned that leadership is about _____

_____

My proudest leadership moment was _____

_____

My next step toward purpose is _____

_____

A challenge I faced recently taught me _____

_____

One Magnus Nugget that spoke to me is _____

_____

I am grateful for _____

_____

I will show gratitude by _____

_____

One person who I can serve better is _____

_____

Journal Page  D ate:_____

---

I learned that leadership is about _____

_____

My proudest leadership moment was _____

_____

My next step toward purpose is _____

_____

A challenge I faced recently taught me _____

_____

One Magnus Nugget that spoke to me is _____

_____

I am grateful for _____

_____

I will show gratitude by _____

_____

One person who I can serve better is _____

_____

**Journal Page**  Date:_____

I learned that leadership is about _____

_____

My proudest leadership moment was _____

_____

My next step toward purpose is _____

_____

A challenge I faced recently taught me _____

_____

One Magnus Nugget that spoke to me is _____

_____

I am grateful for _____

_____

I will show gratitude by _____

_____

One person who I can serve better is _____

_____

**Final Magnus Words**

Thank you for walking this journey with me. May this book serve as a reminder that your leadership matters, your story has value, and your service leaves a legacy.

❖ Lead with humility.
❖ Serve with excellence.
❖ Love without condition.

Because at the end of the day: Magnus Leadership isn't just who we are; it's what we do.

## About the Author

Dr. Michael A. Cadore Sr. is a husband, father, community leader, and lifelong servant of purpose.

A former NFL draftee of the New Orleans Saints and member of the WLAF Montreal Machine, Dr. Cadore turned athletic discipline into lifelong community service.

After three decades in law enforcement, where his leadership earned national recognition, he now serves as Executive Director of Community Engagement & External Affairs at Eastern Florida State College, a board-ready leader with Launch Credit Union, and a Rockledge City Council Member.

Acting on the concept of building legacy of service and continuity, Dr. Cadore was compelled to run for a seat on the Rockledge City Council. In 2019, he was elected to the Rockledge City Council, Seat 1. A seat held with distinction for 36 years by his lifelong mentor, the honorable Dr. Joe Lee Smith. Stepping into that seat was more than an election victory; it was an affirmation of generational service, leadership integrity, and community trust. Dr. Cadore stood on the shoulders of a man who shaped the very heart of Rockledge, and carried such responsibility with gratitude and purpose.

In the municipal election, he earned 2,729 votes (61.94%), a decisive margin which reflected the community's belief in his character, previous accomplishments, and servant-leadership ethos. In the two elections that followed, he ran unopposed, which spoke even louder; not about popularity, but about trust. When a community feels your heart, your work, and your consistency, it responds with unity.

Service during his tenure has included:

• Reviving and strengthening the Student Advisory Council, giving young people a platform to grow, lead, and contribute.

• Supporting and partnering with Aging Matters in Brevard, ensuring our seniors receive dignity, care, and community connection.

• Participating in and promoting 5K races, school fundraisers, and youth enrichment initiatives, expanding opportunities for our students.

• Coordinating food drives and community resource events to uplift families in need.

• Championing fiscal responsibility, strategic planning, and teamwork to strengthen Rockledge's long-term stability.

This work aligns directly with the city's mission:

"Preserving the past and planning the future."

-City of Rockledge's Motto

Dr. Cadore serves knowing that leadership is never a position. Leadership is a responsibility. And he serves with this ethos guiding his footsteps:

"If you don't serve your community now, don't expect your community to serve you later."

Operating in the Magnus Mindset, Mr. Cadore has inspired thousands of students, leaders, and citizens to lead with compassion and conviction.

## Letters from Cadoreables

### Madam Queen Cornelia

To my husband, my Sir King, your leadership, love, and legacy have transformed not just our family, but everyone blessed to know you. I've watched you pour into others selflessly, guiding, mentoring, and inspiring generations to walk in purpose. At an early age, you were taught that serving and being kind to others go a long way. You never look for anything in return; you truly have JOY in helping others, and because of that, your gifts are multiplied in the earth.

The word of God states that two are better than one, because they have a good reward for their labour (*see* Ecclesiastes 4:9 KJV). Through prayer, patience, and praise, we've built a love that stands the test of time and a family that is the heart of our journey together.

I am forever proud of you and honored to walk this journey called life with you as your wife. I thank God for you every day. Honey, please always remember and never forget that I believe in you, and you did so good.

-I love you

## Sir Michael II

Dad, you've been my coach, my compass, and my example of manhood. You've shown me that leadership starts at home and extends into every corner of life. I've watched you serve others even when tired, smile even when tested, and believe even when the odds seemed impossible.

You taught me that being a man of God means standing firm in faith, treating people with respect, and staying humble no matter how high you rise. Because of you, I know that strength and compassion can coexist. And that persistence powered by prayer always wins.

"Have I not commanded you? Be strong and of good courage; do not be afraid, nor be dismayed, for the Lord your God is with you wherever you go."

-Joshua 1:9

## Princess Courtney

Dad, your strength, humility, and unwavering faith have been the foundation of our family. You have shown me that leadership is not just about speaking, it's about serving with sincerity. Watching you lead in our home, in the community, and in your calling has taught me that true greatness is found in consistency and compassion.

You have always reminded us to prepare before we perform and to honor God in all that we do. Because of your example, I strive to carry myself with grace, confidence, and purpose, knowing that leadership is not a position, it's a posture of the heart.

Let your light so shine before men, that they may see your good works, and glorify your Father which is in heaven.

-Matthew 5:16 KJV

## Princess Cierra

Dr. Dad,

Your love has strengthened me in times when I wanted to give up, and your wisdom has guided me when I needed to make decisions. You've shown me that success without faith and service is empty.

You never told me that life would be easy, but you did remind me that if I remember to, "Be bold. Be brave. And be you," I can achieve my wildest dreams. I just have to trust the process and never let anyone outwork me.

> And let us not be weary in well doing: for in due season we shall reap, if we faint not.
>
> -Galatians 6:9 KJV

## About Magnus Solutions Inc.

Magnus Solutions Inc. was founded by Dr. Michael A. Cadore Sr. to educate, encourage, and empower individuals, teams, and communities to live and lead with purpose.

Rooted in the Principles of Success: Preparation, Patience, Professionalism, Pride, Persistence, Praise, Paramount, Respect, Reflection, and Raise; Magnus

Solutions equips people to turn values into action and action into lasting impact.

## Our Mission

To develop servant leaders who transform families, workplaces, and communities through character, consistency, and compassion.

## What We Do

- ❖ Keynote Talks & Conference Addresses (inspirational story-driven leadership messages)
- ❖ Workshops & Trainings (practical skills-based sessions for schools, colleges, businesses, and public agencies)
- ❖ Executive & Team Coaching (targeted development for leaders and high-potential teams)
- ❖ Youth & Collegiate Programs (mentorship, career readiness, and life-skills rooted in service and excellence)
- ❖ Community Engagement Strategy (partnership building, outreach design, and civic impact planning)

## Our Distinctives

- ❖ Servant Leadership First (people over position, impact over image)
- ❖ Faith-Informed Values (integrity, gratitude, and respect at the core)
- ❖ Action Frameworks (simple tools that move audiences from inspiration to implementation)

## Connect with Us

Magnus Solutions Inc.

🌐 www.magnussi.com

✉ info@magnussi.com

Book Dr. Cadore for your next event or training and bring the Principles of Success to life in your organization.

## Community Spotlight Acknowledgments
## The Leaders Who Raised Me

Leadership is not developed alone. Leadership is shaped by the people who influence your character, discipline, heart, and purpose. This section honors the mentors, guides, and leaders whose examples played a defining role in my journey from Titusville to collegiate athletics, professional football, law enforcement, higher education, and community service.

These individuals: my brother Jeff Davis, Dr. Joe Lee Smith, Coach Werneke, Coach Garcia, Coach Kidd, and Jack Parker, shaped my character, sharpened my discipline, elevated my purpose, and strengthened my service.

They stand among the pillars of influence who built the Magnus Mindset.

### Jeff Davis,
### My Brother, My Protector, My Early Hero

My oldest brother, Jeff Davis, has always been more than family. Jeff has always been one of my greatest heroes. Long before the world called me a leader, Jeff showed me what leadership looked like up close. He was the protector who watched over me, the example who stood before me, and the quiet force who shaped the man I would become.

Jeff carried himself with strength that wasn't loud but was always present. His discipline, responsibility, and courage set the Cadore standard in our home. Many of the values I teach today; integrity, respect, consistency, and humility, were first demonstrated by Jeff in everyday life.

He protected me, guided me, and showed me how to be a man long before I understood what manhood required. He didn't need attention to influence. His presence was powerful enough. Jeff taught me that leadership begins with character, and that quiet leadership is still leadership.

He is and will always be one of my first and greatest role models. My brother. My protector. My early hero. My lifelong example of strength.

## Dr. Joe Lee Smith,
## Lifelong Mentor

Dr. Joe Lee Smith, councilman, educator, and historic Brevard County leader, has been a lifelong mentor who shaped my commitment to service, education, community building, and leadership excellence. His guidance has influenced my professional path and my dedication to elevating the next generation.

### Coach Al Werneke,
### Athletic Mentor-Titusville High School

Coach Werneke shaped my discipline, accountability, and championship mindset through a culture built on excellence.

### Coach Jose Garcia,
### Athletic Mentor-Titusville Little League Football

Coach Garcia gave me foundational confidence and early leadership through effort, humility, and teamwork.

### Coach Roy Kidd,
### Athletic Mentor-Eastern Kentucky University

Coach Kidd, a Hall-of-Fame coach, who refined my mental toughness, preparation, performance consistency, and championship discipline.

### Jack Parker,
### Professional Leadership Influence

Jack Parker, two-time former Sheriff of Brevard County and currently Vice President of External Affairs at Eastern Florida State College, has been a significant leadership influence. His example in public safety, professionalism, strategic thinking, and institutional leadership helped strengthen my approach as a servant leader in higher education and community engagement.

---

The section below is for you to acknowledge the leaders who have supported, inspired, and/or journeyed with you.

"A leader is only as strong as the
community that stands with them."

Name: _____

Organization: _____

### Impact or Lesson:

Name: _____

Organization: _____

### Impact or Lesson:

Name: _____
Organization: _____

### Impact or Lesson:

Name: _____
Organization: _____

### Impact or Lesson:

Name: _____
Organization: _____

### Impact or Lesson:

Name: _____

Organization: _____

### Impact or Lesson:


---

Name: _____

Organization: _____

### Impact or Lesson:


---

Name: _____

Organization: _____

### Impact or Lesson:

# Part IV:
# Magnus Expansion Pack

# Magnus Vision & Growth Workbook

# Table of Contents

## Getting Started

A common question I am asked is, "How can I grow as a leader?" Throughout this book, I have shared personal stages of development around significant life events. You can know my story and recite each Principle of Success yet remain stagnant. Advancement only comes with forward momentum. This requires more than talking and writing, it requires intentional consistent action.

Today, identify your starting point: *Where do you come from (i.e. biological family, mindset, stage of life, etc.)?* Articulate your purpose: *Why serve beyond yourself?* Look ahead at your legacy: *How can you leave the standard higher?*

_____

_____

_____

_____

_____

_____

_____

_____

_____

## Legacy Preparation

Self-Assessment: Rate yourself from 1–5
(1 = Needs Improvement to 5 = Strong):

**Identity:** Do I know who I am and what shaped me?

**Rating:** _____ **Why?** _____

_____

**Purpose:** Am I serving beyond myself daily?

**Rating:** _____ **Why?** _____

_____

**Legacy:** Am I building something that outlives me?

**Rating:** _____ **Why?** _____

_____

**Discipline:** Are my habits aligned with my goals?

**Rating:** _____ **Why?** _____

_____

**Leadership:** Do I elevate others through my actions?

**Rating:** _____ **Why?** _____

_____

**Community:** Am I strengthening the world around me?

**Rating:** _____ **Why?** _____

_____

Legacy is the heartbeat of the Magnus Mindset. It determines what remains long after the applause fades. My legacy begins with my family: My Queen, Cornelia, and our children, Princess Courtney, Princess Cierra, and Sir Michael II. They are my reason, my motivation, and my accountability.

My legacy extends to:

- ❖ The students I support
- ❖ The young men I mentor
- ❖ The community programs I build
- ❖ The families I serve
- ❖ The institutions I strengthen
- ❖ The leaders I help develop

Legacy is not what you leave when life is over; legacy is what you build daily.

## Six Lenses of the Magnus Mindset

1. *The Champion Mindset:* Built through discipline, consistency, and adversity on and off the field.

2. *The Servant Leader Mindset:* The commitment to place people and purpose above ego.

3. *The Public Catalytic Servant Mindset:* Serving with integrity, empathy, and emotional discipline to watch others grow and succeed.

4. *The Educator & Community Mindset:* Building opportunities, partnerships, and impact.

5. *The Governance Mindset:* Thinking long-term, stewarding resources, and protecting community.

6. *The Family Mindset:* Leading your home with love, unity, and accountability.

## Principles in Action

The upcoming pages will help you move from learning to living the ten Principles of Success. Leadership is not found in the spotlight, but in the shadows where service happens. Review each principle in Part I of this book as you reflect:

### Preparation is the quiet rehearsal before destiny's performance.

✓ One habit I will strengthen this week:

_____

_____

✓ A challenge I will prepare for ahead of time:

_____

_____

✓ Someone who models strong preparation:

_____

_____

## Patience is faith stretched across time.

✓ A situation where I need more patience:

_____

_____

✓ A lesson this season is teaching me:

_____

_____

✓ Waiting well can improve my leadership by:

_____

_____

## Professionalism is consistency
## when no one applauds.

✓ One area where I can raise my standards:

_____

_____

✓ A relationship that needs professionalism restored:

_____

_____

✓ I will model excellence for others by:

_____

_____

## Pride is gratitude dressed in discipline.

✓ An accomplishment I am most grateful for:

_____

_____

✓ I represent my community with honor by:

_____

_____

✓ I show humility while being confident by:

_____

_____


## Persistence is courage wearing work boots.

✓ A goal that still matters most to me:

_____

_____

✓ A person who inspires me not to give up is:

_____

_____

✓ A daily routine that helps me keep momentum is:

_____

_____

## Praise transforms a workplace into a worship space.

✓ A person who deserves my public appreciation:

_____

_____

✓ A way I can celebrate progress, not just perfection:

_____

_____

✓ Today, I thank God for the blessing of:

_____

_____


## Purpose without people becomes pride.

✓ Something that truly matters at this time in my life:

_____

_____

✓ Ways I will align my calendar with my calling:

_____

_____

✓ People who benefit from my sense of purpose are:

_____

_____

## Respect is the currency
## that never loses value.

✓ A person's whose perspective I should listen to more intentionally is:

_____

_____

✓ An example of modeling respect during conflict:

_____

_____

✓ Habits that help me honor myself and others:

_____

_____

## Reflection turns memory into mastery.

✓ The event that taught me the most this quarter:

_____

_____

✓ I grew from that experience by:

_____

_____

✓ Next time I will:

_____

_____

## *To raise others is to repay the blessings that raised you.*

✓ Currently, I am mentoring:

_____

_____

✓ Specific ways I can help them grow are:

_____

_____

✓ Raising others strengthens my own leadership by:

_____

_____

## 12-Month Magnus Vision & Growth Planner

Use this section as a journal to document the steps you take and the progress you make over the next 12 months. Reflect on your experiences, recording any changes, challenges, or insights you gain along the way. Please don't skip ahead. Remember, meaningful change takes time. Celebrate each small step forward and trust that your efforts will lead to lasting results. Time moves at the same pace everywhere in the world, for everyone, universally, and can't be rushed.

# Month 1: Identity

Know who you are before the world tells you
who to be creates the foundation for greatness.

-Carl Jung[1]

**Theme:** Know who you are!

## Key Questions:

1. What is my vision for this month?
2. What is one habit I will strengthen?
3. What is one obstacle I will prepare for this month?
4. What am I learning about myself this month?
5. What habits or actions align with this month's focus?
6. What is one challenge I must overcome?
7. What is one strength I must develop further?

## Action Steps:

1. Choose 3 practical steps to practice this month.
2. Track your progress weekly.
3. Record your insights in the reflection section.

[1]"TOP 25 QUOTES by CARL JUNG (of 822) | A-Z Quotes." A-Z Quotes, 2009, www.azquotes
.com/author/7659-Carl_Jung.

_____

_____

_____

_____

# End of the Month Action Summary

My biggest insight this month:

_____

_____

_____

_____

_____

_____

Three actions I will take immediately:

_____

_____

_____

_____

_____

People who I will share the Magnus Leadership
Principles of Success with:

_____

_____

_____

_____

_____

# Month 2: Discipline

Master your habits, master your life.

-Dr. Myles Munroe[1]

**Theme:** Develop mastery.

## Key Questions:

1. What am I waiting for that requires faith?
2. How can I use this waiting season productively?
3. What am I learning about myself this month?
4. What habits or actions align with this month's focus?
5. What is one challenge I must overcome?
6. What is one strength I must develop further?

## Action Steps:

1. Choose 3 practical steps to practice this month.
2. Track your progress weekly.
3. Record your insights in the reflection section.

[1]The Chosen Path. "Master Your Habits, Master Your Life | Dr. Myles Munroe." YouTube, 3 Aug. 2025, www.youtube.com/watch?v=tSZM1jImAMc. Accessed 20 Dec. 2025.

_____

_____

_____

_____

_____

# End of the Month Action Summary

My biggest insight this month:

_____
_____
_____
_____
_____

Three actions I will take immediately:

_____
_____
_____
_____

People who I will share the Magnus Leadership Principles of Success with:

_____
_____
_____
_____
_____

# Month 3: Purpose

Clarify why you exist and
who you are called to serve.

**Theme:** Seek clarity.

## Key Questions:
1. How did I demonstrate integrity this week?
2. What relationship can I improve with respect?
3. What am I learning about myself this month?
4. What habits or actions align with this month's focus?
5. What is one challenge I must overcome?
6. What is one strength I must develop further?

## Action Steps:
1. Choose 3 practical steps to practice this month.
2. Track your progress weekly.
3. Record your insights in the reflection section.

_____

_____

_____

_____

_____

## End of the Month Action Summary

My biggest insight this month:

_____
_____
_____
_____
_____
_____

Three actions I will take immediately:

_____
_____
_____
_____
_____

People who I will share the Magnus Leadership Principles of Success with:

_____
_____
_____
_____
_____

# Month 4: Service

Lead by giving more than you take.

-Steven M. Huskey[1]

**Theme:** Be a servant leader.

## Key Questions:

1. How did I demonstrate self-respect and gratitude this month?
2. How do I represent my family name and legacy?
3. What is one thing I will do with excellence this month?
4. What am I learning about myself this month?
5. What habits or actions align with this month's focus?
6. What is one challenge I must overcome?
7. What is one strength I must develop further?

## Action Steps:

1. Choose 3 practical steps to practice this month.
2. Track your progress weekly.
3. Record your insights in the reflection section.

[1]Huskey, Steven M. "The Art of Abundance: Giving Back More than You Take - the Excelerated Life." The Excelerated Life, 25 Jan. 2024, theexceleratedlife.com/the-art-of-abundance/. Accessed 28 Dec. 2025.

## End of the Month Action Summary

My biggest insight this month:

_____

_____

_____

_____

_____

_____

Three actions I will take immediately:

_____

_____

_____

_____

_____

People who I will share the Magnus Leadership Principles of Success with:

_____

_____

_____

_____

_____

_____

# Month 5: Professionalism

Show excellence in every environment.

**Theme:** Develop a reputation of excellence.

## Key Questions:

1. When people hear my name, what do they expect in regard to work ethic?
2. What actions can I take to produce greater excellence in a specific area of my life?
3. What is one habit I will develop to ensure excellence?
4. What am I learning about myself this month?
5. What habits or actions align with this month's focus?
6. What is one challenge I must overcome?
7. What is one strength I must develop further?

## Action Steps:

1. Choose 3 practical steps to practice this month.
2. Track your progress weekly.
3. Record your insights in the reflection section.

_____

_____

_____

## End of the Month Action Summary

My biggest insight this month:

_____
_____
_____
_____
_____

Three actions I will take immediately:

_____
_____
_____
_____
_____

People who I will share the Magnus Leadership Principles of Success with:

_____
_____
_____
_____
_____

## Month 6: Patience

Trust the process, even when progress isn't visible.

**Theme:** Keep a legacy focus.

### Key Questions:

1. What goal is taking longer than I expected to manifest?
2. How has my expectation changed during the development process?
3. What are some lessons I am learning while waiting?
4. What am I learning about myself this month?
5. What habits or actions align with this month's focus?
6. What is one challenge I must overcome?
7. What is one strength I must develop further?

### Action Steps:

1. Choose 3 practical steps to practice this month.
2. Track your progress weekly.
3. Record your insights in the reflection section.

---

## End of the Month Action Summary

My biggest insight this month:

_____

_____

_____

_____

_____

Three actions I will take immediately:

_____

_____

_____

_____

_____

People who I will share the Magnus Leadership
Principles of Success with:

_____

_____

_____

_____

_____

## Month 7: Persistence

Stay committed when it gets difficult.

**Theme:** Hold on to the vision.

### Key Questions:
1. What challenges have I overcome in the past that are now helping me with this difficulty?
2. What will I miss out on if I give up now?
3. What advice do I give others when they are faced with challenges?
4. What am I learning about myself this month?
5. What habits or actions align with this month's focus?
6. What is one challenge I must overcome?
7. What is one strength I must develop further?

### Action Steps:
1. Choose 3 practical steps to practice this month.
2. Track your progress weekly.
3. Record your insights in the reflection section.

_____

_____

_____

_____

## End of the Month Action Summary

My biggest insight this month:

_____

_____

_____

_____

_____

_____

Three actions I will take immediately:

_____

_____

_____

_____

_____

People who I will share the Magnus Leadership Principles of Success with:

_____

_____

_____

_____

_____

_____

## Month 8: Respect

Honor every place, person, and opportunity.

**Theme:** Sowing and reaping respect.

### Key Questions:
1. How has disrespect limited me in the past?
2. How has respect elevated me?
3. How do others rate my level of respect in various settings?
4. What am I learning about myself this month?
5. What habits or actions align with this month's focus?
6. What is one challenge I must overcome?
7. What is one strength I must develop further?

### Action Steps:
1. Choose 3 practical steps to practice this month.
2. Track your progress weekly.
3. Record your insights in the reflection section.

_____

_____

_____

_____

_____

## End of the Month Action Summary

My biggest insight this month:

_____

_____

_____

_____

_____

Three actions I will take immediately:

_____

_____

_____

_____

People who I will share the Magnus Leadership
Principles of Success with:

_____

_____

_____

_____

_____

## Month 9: Reflection

Review, refine, and reset your direction.

**Theme:** No one is perfect, but everyone can be perfected.

### Key Questions:
1. What area of my life am I the most successful?
2. What area of my life needs the biggest reset?
3. How can I refine certain habits to produce better outcomes?
4. What am I learning about myself this month?
5. What habits or actions align with this month's focus?
6. What is one challenge I must overcome?
7. What is one strength I must develop further?

### Action Steps:
1. Choose 3 practical steps to practice this month.
2. Track your progress weekly.
3. Record your insights in the reflection section.

_____

_____

_____

_____

## End of the Month Action Summary

My biggest insight this month:

_____

_____

_____

_____

_____

Three actions I will take immediately:

_____

_____

_____

_____

_____

People who I will share the Magnus Leadership Principles of Success with:

_____

_____

_____

_____

_____

# Month 10: Community Engagement

Elevate the world around you.

**Theme:** Network increase net worth!

## Key Questions:
1. What community projects have I been a part of in the past that have impacted others?
2. How can I use my gifts to better serve my community?
3. What are some ways I can benefit from the influence and/or support of others?
4. What am I learning about myself this month?
5. What habits or actions align with this month's focus?
6. What is one challenge I must overcome?
7. What is one strength I must develop further?

## Action Steps:
1. Choose 3 practical steps to practice this month.
2. Track your progress weekly.
3. Record your insights in the reflection section.

_____

_____

_____

## End of the Month Action Summary

My biggest insight this month:

_____

_____

_____

_____

_____

Three actions I will take immediately:

_____

_____

_____

_____

_____

People who I will share the Magnus Leadership Principles of Success with:

_____

_____

_____

_____

_____

## Month 11: Leadership Presence

Show up with confidence, clarity, and character.

**Theme:** I *know* I can!

### Key Questions:

1. How did I build confidence in a previous area of weakness?
2. What do I need to gain a better understanding of to become more confident?
3. In what areas of my life do I need to gain clarity (be truthful with myself) to improve my character?
4. What am I learning about myself this month?
5. What habits or actions align with this month's focus?
6. What is one challenge I must overcome?
7. What is one strength I must develop further?

### Action Steps:

1. Choose 3 practical steps to practice this month.
2. Track your progress weekly.
3. Record your insights in the reflection section.

_____

_____

_____

## End of the Month Action Summary

My biggest insight this month:

_____
_____
_____
_____
_____

Three actions I will take immediately:

_____
_____
_____
_____

People who I will share the Magnus Leadership
Principles of Success with:

_____
_____
_____
_____
_____

# Month 12: Legacy Building

Build something that lasts beyond you.

**Theme:** Setting a generational mindset.

## Key Questions:

1. What impact am I making for my children, grandchildren, and beyond?
2. What lasting benefit am I creating for my community?
3. What do people think of when they hear my name?
4. What am I learning about myself this month?
5. What habits or actions align with this month's focus?
6. What is one challenge I must overcome?
7. What is one strength I must develop further?

## Action Steps:

1. Choose 3 practical steps to practice this month.
2. Track your progress weekly.
3. Record your insights in the reflection section.

---

## End of the Month Action Summary

My biggest insight this month:

_____

_____

_____

_____

_____

_____

Three actions I will take immediately:

_____

_____

_____

_____

_____

_____

People who I will share the Magnus Leadership Principles of Success with:

_____

_____

_____

_____

_____

_____

**Extended Legacy Letters**

I invite you to write a personal "Legacy Letter." Below are a few suggestions.

Prompt 1:

Write a letter to your younger self, describing the leader you've become and the lessons you would share.

Prompt 2:

Write a letter to someone you are mentoring. Encourage them to live by the Magnus Principles.

Prompt 3:

Write a letter to your community, church, or organization outlining how you intend to serve them over the next decade.

_____

_____

_____

_____

_____

_____

_____

_____

_____

## Closing Invocation

"Lord, guide my hands to serve, my heart to love, and my mind to lead."

As you close this journal, remember that Magnus Leadership is not a destination; it is a lifestyle.

## MAGNUS SOLUTIONS, INC.
"Not just good ideas, but MAGNUS SOLUTIONS!"

"If you don't serve your community now, don't expect your community to serve you later."

- Michael A. Cadore, Ed. D
Founder & President
Magnus Solutions, Inc

# Autographs

www.ingramcontent.com/pod-product-compliance
Lightning Source LLC
Chambersburg PA
CBHW071725120626
46550CB00002B/393